What's There to Write About?

KALLI DAKOS

Scholastic

Scholastic-TAB Publications Ltd.
123 Newkirk Road, Richmond Hill, Ontario, Canada L4C 3G5

Scholastic Inc.
730 Broadway, New York, NY 10003, USA

Ashton Scholastic Pty Limited
PO Box 579, Gosford, NSW 2250, Australia

Ashton Scholastic Limited
165 Marua Road, Panmure, Auckland 6, New Zealand

Scholastic Publications Ltd.
Holly Walk, Leamington Spa, Warwickshire CV324LS, England

Cover design by Yüksel Hassan
With special thanks to Aisha Hassan
Cover photographed by Marilyn Rumble
Edited by Dyanne Rivers

7 6 5 4 3 2 1 Printed in the USA 9/80123/9

Canadian Cataloguing in Publication Data

Dakos, Kalli

ISBN 0-590-73354-0

1. Creative writing (Elementary education) — Study and teaching. 2. Creative writing (Elementary education) — Problems, exercises, etc. I. Title

LB1576.D33   1989   372.6'23   C89-093442-8

To the children
at Manlius Pebble Hill School,
Braddock Elementary School
and Forestville Elementary School
who taught me to celebrate
the moments in our classrooms
and helped me discover
the most important stories of all.

Foreword

*I stared and stared at my blank piece of paper. All the
other kids have ideas but I don't, so I have to stay after school.*
*I sat for an hour and a half to figure out what to write
about. Then a kid said, "I have advice. Write what you feel."*
So I did.
Then I went home and waited.
I thought I would get an F.
But I got an A.
I thank my friend.

John, Grade 4

As a child, I dreamed of becoming a teacher. But I also wanted
to be a writer, and for much of my life I have felt pulled by these
two forces.

When I was a classroom teacher, I often jotted down notes, kept
diaries and wrote stories and plays for my students, hoping that, at
some point, I would be able to pursue writing seriously. This desire
lurked like a shadow at the back of my mind until I took a
sabbatical from teaching.

For a few years, I studied news reporting and covered stories for
a local newspaper. I wrote poems and short articles for children's
magazines on topics from seat-belt safety to life in Inuvik, a
community in Canada's Northwest Territories, magazine articles
for parenting and educational publications and short pieces of
fiction for my daughter's nursery school classes. I even tried my
hand at storytelling.

But writing is a lonely, solitary profession and before long I
ached for the classroom, for children and adults to share my days
with. I have always loved the excitement of the elementary school
world, and knew I was a fish out of water at my word processor
every day.

My story really begins on the day I returned to school after my
years as a writer. I was totally unprepared for the gold mine of
stories I would soon discover right in my own classroom.

I can still see my students on that first day — Johnathon with his solemn, dark brown eyes, nervous and afraid because this was his first day in a new school; Sandra, who drew squiggles in the shapes of arms and legs all over the numbers in her math book; and Christy, who kept asking, "What time is it? Is my daddy ever going to come and take me home?"

Even the teachers had their own stories. Ms. Randy had transferred from a high school and was nervously ready to tackle the frontiers of second grade. I was the new reading teacher and I could hardly wait to share my stories, poems and articles with my students.

That evening, when I sat down at my computer to begin writing, the words, images and stories flowed like a river in spring. As I covered page after page, I realized I had been a part of hundreds of stories that very day. The teachers and students in my new school were characters working on the chapters of their lives, and I had played a part in their stories. This book tells the story of how I stumbled across this exciting discovery.

Embedded in the daily routines of the school and classroom, there is a rich world of ideas and feelings. It's a world we often take for granted, but it can become quite extraordinary when we begin to look at it through a writer's eyes.

What is described is not so much a program as a way of looking at the classroom and, indeed, at life in all its dimensions. Once teachers and students begin to see that they are surrounded by stories, they will never again need to ask, "What's there to write about?"

Kalli Dakos
Great Falls, Virginia

The ordinary becomes extraordinary

In the years I spent working as a writer, I had begun to look at the world through an artist's eyes. I tell my students that an artist uses:

His eyes to see.
His ears to hear.
His mind to think.
His heart to feel.
His imagination to soar.

If you can't laugh and cry and be moved by the stories of others, you will never be a writer. All artists wear glasses with lenses that help them embrace life and see the richness in daily routines.

It was these lenses that led me to my first stories about the elementary school world.

Michelle was a very quiet first grader, already working well below grade level. She had the greatest difficulty with math and dreaded the subject like a visit to the dentist. One day, I had withdrawn her from class to work on diagnostic testing, and when I said we were finished she looked at me aghast. "Not so soon," she pleaded. "Please give me some more tests. I don't want to go back until math is finished."

"Why?" I asked, noticing the almost desperate look in her eyes.

"Because math is trouble! Trouble! Trouble!"

There was rhythm in her words, and I could feel it. There was also passion and pain and I could sympathize because I, too, always dreaded mathematics. Michelle's pain compelled me to write "Math is Brewing and I'm in Trouble." This poem begins:

Numbers single,
Numbers double,
Math is brewing,
And I'm in trouble,
If I could mix a magic brew,
Numbers I'd take care of you.
You'd disappear far in the air,
And I'd be left without a care.

I always think of Michelle when I reread this poem. It was not my job to help her with mathematics, and I hope she has found a teacher to help unlock the secret of numbers for her.

I do know, however, how she felt after I read this poem. She was in awe of the words and the rhythm that expressed how she felt. Above all, she was honored to be the inspiration for a poem that rapidly became a favorite in our school.

When I first began my teaching career, I would have missed the passion and rhythm in the words "Trouble! Trouble! Trouble!" Michelle was telling me her story and, through my writing, I discovered it was also my story and the story of many of my students.

It is the job of the artist to transform these ordinary events into special words and rhythms that become extraordinary in their power. We are surrounded by stories like these every day in our classrooms, which are filled with the wonderful, happy, sad, tragic and sometimes incredible tales of our students. When I returned to teaching, it was as if the blinders had been taken off my eyes. The stories were everywhere. There was always something to write about.

The day Maria, a first grader, forgot her lunch on the school bus and told me her tale of woe, I wrote:

I forgot my lunch on the school bus,
I'm in such a state of dismay,
My lunch is still on the school bus,
And the bus has driven away.
Who will I tell?
What will I say?
What a horrible way to start the day!

Another day, I was eating lunch with a group of second **graders** when we heard a scream from Allison. "There's a pickle in my soup!" she yelled.

Immediately, I sensed I was in the middle of a story. Here is an excerpt from it. (Remember, I wrote about what I saw. The children provided the words as the story unfolded right in front of me.)

Tell the principal, there's a pickle in Allison's soup.
Does anyone else's soup have a pickle in it?
Maybe they made a mistake in the kitchen today, and
started putting pickles in all the soup.

One day, I was working in a second-grade classroom when I heard the teacher yell at Eric, "You must stop doing that. It's not good for you to eat paste!"

I couldn't believe my ears, so I went over to him. "Why are you eating paste?" I asked.

"Just for something to do," he told me.

Then I asked, "Eric, can you imagine what your insides are going to look like if you keep eating this stuff?"

"No!" he replied.

"Do you mind if I write about it?" I asked.

"Sure, go ahead," he nodded.

The title of this poem became "Does Eric Know What he Ate Today?" Here is part of it.

The doctors will be shocked to see,
How stuck your insides came to be.
Your esophagus will be glued to your heart,
And your stomach and liver will not part,
And with bowels stuck to kidneys, you'll see,
How awful eating paste can be.

In just about every primary classroom I have visited, there is at least one student who eats paste. I may be the only teacher who has ever written about it.

Today, I would use this episode with Eric to spark writing activities. I would be interested in his opinions and those of other class members. But when it happened, I was still the only one writing. Though my students were listening to my stories and poems, they had not yet begun to write their own.

Capturing special moments forever

It took a while for the significance of my stories and poems to sink in. I knew the children loved them and I did too. But I didn't understand everything that was operating as we shared our experiences.

When I wrote the poems about Michelle, Maria, Allison and Eric, I was transforming apparently ordinary, everyday classroom events into special moments we would never forget. The children loved to read and reread these poems. They wanted to illustrate them, share them with parents and dramatize them in front of the entire school. They were thrilled whenever I suggested that one of their experiences would make an interesting poem or story.

We began enjoying our classroom experiences even more, because we were always on the lookout for special moments. My students were beginning to see, with an artist's eyes, the power of the written word to transform the ordinary into the extraordinary.

The children begin to write

In our school, creative writing was taught separately from reading and literature. Basal readers were still used extensively and, as the reading teacher, this left me little time to pursue writing and reading within the context of whole language — or so I thought.

It was the children who began showing me the way. They would race up to me in the hall with a scrap of paper and say, "I know a story! It's a great one! It happened in spelling!" Or they would bounce into my classroom asking, "Do you need any ideas for a story? Lots has been happening today!" Often at lunch, as we were having our discussions, a student would pipe up, as if a light bulb had just gone on in his or her head, "Hey, you could write a story about that!"

One day Brian came to school with a piece of special paper. "It's my story," he told me. "I wrote it in my brain in arithmetic yesterday. It was so hot that I couldn't concentrate and my hands were all sweaty. I started dreaming of what I would do if I only had a wish. When I got home I wrote it on paper."

I looked at the paper. The story was titled "The Flying Class." I still have that piece of paper, because it symbolizes the start of my new writing program. Brian wrote, not because he was asked to, not for marks or gold stars, but because he wanted to. He was writing like a real artist. He had created something special that he felt compelled to share. His story begins:

Our hands felt wet and sticky
On our arithmetic test.
It was getting too hot to concentrate
And we all needed fresh air.
When Ms. Madison went next door,
To speak with the kindergarten teacher
We got a screwdriver from the janitor
And used it to take
The window out of the classroom.
Then we all flew out,
Knowing children can fly
If they want to.

My students joined Brian and me and we all began writing stories about our lives. When Jonah lost a tooth or Danny was forgotten at the listening center or Terry finally passed a spelling test, we celebrated by writing about it.

We began noticing everything. Ryan always came to class with his shoelaces untied. "Twenty-two Stitches" was written in his honor.

Once there was a boy named Ryan, and he always had his shoelaces untied.
One day, he tripped on his laces in the hall. The ambulance was called because he hurt his leg badly. He was rushed to the hospital. The doctors had to operate.
When Ryan came back he had twenty-two stitches on his leg.

When Rajneesh finally passed an arithmetic test, he wrote a story called "The Best Day of my Life." It said, "I had all the math answers right. All sixteen of them. That's why I am so happy."

One day a mother brought a giant submarine sandwich to school as a special treat for her son's birthday. The sheer size of that sandwich sparked imaginations and the stories flowed — titles ranged from "The Biggest, Hugest Sandwich in the World" to "The Sandwich That Could Not Be Eaten."

Another day, Charles came to school with a container of strange fruit in his lunch box. He would not eat it, he said, until he knew what it was.

"I know what it is," a third grader piped up. "It's an unidentified floating object."

And so another story based on an event that really happened in our classroom was born — the day Charles came to school with lichee fruit.

Sharing feelings

My enthusiasm for the drama of the elementary school world was obviously contagious — my students were seeing and writing the stories of their lives, for the pure joy of it. Unwittingly, we had stumbled onto a marvelous form of communication, one that was spreading its magic. And when they realized they would be taken seriously, the children became free to express their genuine feelings and emotions.

Early in the year, I asked them to criticize and evaluate my work. Did I get the story right? Would children like it? How could I improve it?

I never encountered a more enthusiastic group of editors. Often, as I tried to understand the children's point of view or their reasons for doing something, I would say, "I need you to help me understand. I was a child a long time ago and the world is a different place today. In order to write about this interesting idea, I need to know how you feel and think about it."

As they realized that their thoughts and emotions were valued, the children's confidence began to grow. And I began to appreciate my own position as a writer and elementary school teacher, a person working on the front lines of education. Researchers, principals, superintendents and evaluators all stood behind the other teachers and me on this line.

Teachers are as close to children as the blankets they snuggle up with in bed every night. We work with them on a day-to-day basis. We see them happy, sad, frustrated, disgruntled, angry and tired. We know how they respond to the curriculum that has been developed for them, where it works and where it doesn't. It became important to me to report from those front lines all I was learning, and to value my thoughts and opinions enough to share them.

So many children today have no one to talk to, no one to share their inner world with. It seems to me that teachers, parents and administrators are often on such a fast-paced carousel that we are in danger of missing what is really important. Events whiz by so quickly that everything ends up out of focus.

The writing provided an opportunity for me and the children to slow down. We took time to savor special moments, to write about them, think about them and hold them in our hands. I was able to catch glimpses of what lay in my students' hearts and to sort out what is truly important in my work as a teacher.

Every child, no matter how bright or competent, how skilled or privileged, has problems in school. The writing gave my students a chance to find the words to express their problems, and thereby to understand them. There is a kind of therapeutic value in writing, even for our youngest children.

I know it helped Monica when she was stuck on the nine-times tables, struggling to memorize them day after day. She expressed her feelings beautifully in her writing.

Nine is awful!
I wish we counted like this.
1 2 3 4 5 6 7 8 10
I'm stuck on nine.
I have lots of other work to do.
And it's time to go.
What should I do?

There was the day Jamie came to reading class, upset that she had been falsely accused of doing something wrong. "I'm in trouble," she told me, "and it isn't fair. This dumb school isn't fair."

I suggested that she write about what had happened. Is there a child anywhere who hasn't experienced Jamie's story?

In my reading group I had to go to my seat and the other kids were able to stay in the reading group. Skip kept kicking the chair and he did not get in trouble. The other kids were doing their work out loud and saying the answers when they shouldn't have, and they did not get in trouble. I was being perfectly good and I got in trouble.

Sometimes the children provided me with the words for my own writing. For example, Tony disappeared from math class one day and I was asked to find him. I finally discovered him hiding in the bathroom. He didn't want to go back to the room because his classmates were calling him names, he hated his arithmetic book and, with a substitute teacher, he felt like "a birdie locked inside a cage."

His words inspired me to write:

I'm hiding in the bathroom,
There's no one here to see,
I'm tired of my schoolwork,
And wish they'd set me free.
Free of that darn math book
And those questions on the page,
I feel like a birdie,
Locked inside a cage.
Free of all those noisy kids,
Rattling around the room,
And calling me such awful names,
I'll never last till June.
Free of that darn substitute
Who screeches and who yells,
The bathroom is the nicest place,
To sit and wait for bells.

I'll never forget a cold, rainy November day when I groaned at the thought of having to take my second graders outside to cross into another building. The rain had just turned to snow as we raced to the other side.

I turned around and couldn't believe my eyes. Terry and Sam were walking with their mouths open, letting the snowflakes land on their tongues and saying how good they tasted. I remember looking at them and wondering how they could be enjoying themselves in such awful weather. Today I'd go back, taste the snowflakes with them and perhaps write about the experience as well.

Another day I was visiting in a school in Toronto when a teacher complained to me that a student had jumped in a giant mud puddle right beside her at recess. Her best dress was covered in brown, muddy blotches. "I'm Sorry, Ms. Digby" was born.

> *Ms. Digby: Jason, just look at this mud on my dress,*
> *You jumped in the puddle and now I'm a mess.*
> *And this red-and-white outfit is my very best.*
> *Jason: I'm sorry, Ms. Digby.*
> *Ms. Digby: I'm sick of your sorries,*
> *Your excuses each day.*
> *Sorry won't make this mess go away.*
> *Jason: I'm sorry, Ms. Digby.*

One day, Mike bent over and split his pants right up the front. His teacher, Mrs. Salisbury, who was not in the habit of writing poetry, was inspired by the muse:

> *Today was an awful day for Mike,*
> *He bent over and got a fright.*
> *His pants had split right up the front,*
> *A giant hole, a great big cut!*
> *"Oh no! What bad luck," he said.*
> *And blushed a bright and shining red,*
> *And even tried to hide his head.*

We enjoyed these poems tremendously. By writing about incidents like these, we communicate a joy in the daily happenings of our lives and use writing as a way of understanding and celebrating them.

Making sense out of life

In her book *Gates of Excellence, On Reading and Writing Books for Children*, Katherine Paterson writes, "...language is not simply the instrument by which we communicate thought. The language we speak will shape the thoughts and feelings themselves."

The children and I soon realized that writing can improve our lives. Through writing, we were able to deal with our emotions and feelings by finding healthy ways to express them.

One day, Alicia and three other students had to sing "Happy Birthday" in a packed auditorium. Just before they went on stage, Alicia was stricken with hiccups and, in a panic, asked, "What am I supposed to do now?" She went on stage.

When we returned to class, I wrote her story. The children loved the chorus:

Happy HICCUP to you
Happy HICCUP to you
Happy birthday, dear HICCUP
Happy HICCUP to you!

This experience could have been embarrassing for Alicia. But when it was written from a humorous point of view, it became a memory to treasure.

Every classroom has at least one dawdler, a student who just can't seem to get the work done. I wondered how this must feel, from the child's point of view, and asked a dawdler for help with this poem. Here are the last two stanzas:

I'm sitting here and thinking
How it ever came to be,
That papers formed a jail cell,
And somehow captured me.
The teacher says I dawdle,
And her words are very true,
But does she know how much I wish,
I'd get the work done too?

My students were in awe of the words that could capture and make sense of such feelings.

Goodbyes are always difficult. My students and I learned that writing helped. Tim was saying goodbye to our small reading group because he had been transferred into a special education class. He wrote about his feelings:

Monday is my last day here.
I will miss my classroom.
I will miss my teacher.
I will miss my friends.
I don't feel good about leaving.

We used Tim's impending transfer to discuss this aspect of life and to write and read more about it. John wrote about his puppy's death, Sarah about leaving her best friend in another city and Jim about giving up his soccer games because he didn't enjoy them anymore.

We write, not only to communicate our thoughts and feelings, but also to make sense out of our lives.

Developing a sense of wonder

When I returned to teaching after my years as a writer, the stories I was privileged to be a part of continually amazed me. Now everything in my school life mattered — every comment from a teacher or child, every incident in the cafeteria or hallway, every story from every angle.

I wrote "Puke! Puke!" when I saw a janitor running down the hall with a mop and bucket in his hands; I wrote "Budging Lineups" when I saw a class pushing and shoving in line one day; I wrote "The Perfect Class" when I had the chance to observe the most imperfect class I have ever seen and wondered what gift I could give its long-suffering teacher. "It's Inside My Sister's Lunch" was inspired by the students' forgetfulness in bringing their book money to school and "Oink! Oink! There's a Pig Inside Our Classroom" when William was pretending he was a pig one day.

My sense of wonder was growing in leaps and bounds and it couldn't help but rub off on my students.

I'll never forget a story a teacher told me. Her class had watched caterpillars shed their skins five times and then observed the chrysalis under the last skin. They waited breathlessly for the butterflies to emerge and open their wings for the first time.

But one butterfly had oddly shaped wings and four legs instead of the normal six. The children watched and waited, hoping this butterfly would not die. One day it did.

They were sad. The same day, they had a writing lesson and most of the children could think of nothing to write about. I find I can't forget this story — of the class that searched for something to write about while a butterfly died at the back of the room. If we want our children to develop a sense of wonder, we must lead the way.

Another teacher, working on the same butterfly unit, did just this. She suggested that the children describe, in writing, their experiences with butterflies. Here are two of their stories:

The day Mrs. Picciano let the painted lady butterflies go, I was filled with mixed emotions. I didn't know if I was supposed to be happy for the butterfly or sad for me.

The butterfly that I got to let go was deformed. When it came time to let them go, my butterfly would not get off my finger. Finally he did, and to this day he is probably still alive.

Today I held a butterfly. It felt scary, fun, neat and nice. Sometimes you just have to go outside and look, feel and smell nature. But have you ever been like your feelings are all locked up inside?

Well, the butterfly is a pretty insect. If your hand touches a butterfly, you'll be full of joy. The butterfly, in my opinion, is the most pretty insect that ever lived.

When I got to hold it, I felt that love touched the heart of me and the butterfly.

14

Learning to savor life

One day I was peacefully eating my tuna salad sandwich in the cafeteria, when I overheard a discussion that soon had me roaring with laughter. Tony was screaming, "Who took a bite out of my sandwich?" The children in his second-grade class were all clamoring, "I didn't! I didn't!" and I heard Melissa say, "You must have taken a bite out of your own sandwich, Tony!"

Finally, the poor teacher stood up and asked, "Who took a bite out of Tony's sandwich?"

At this point, I couldn't control myself anymore, and I burst out laughing.

Did the teacher have any idea of the incredible story that had just fallen into her lap? I wondered about the millions of stories that die before they are given a chance to be born, about the millions of times teachers hold special moments like this in their hands and let them slip away. These moments are fleeting and lost all too quickly. They must be respected and cherished immediately, for all the joy they can give.

Paul Pearsall has identified a branch of psychiatry that he calls joyology. In his book, *Super Joy*, he writes, "This super joy goes far beyond happiness or contentment. It is the regular and enduring celebration of the delight in daily living, the savoring of the moments of life that are all too often missed, eclipsed by our patterned numbness to the thrill of being alive and being human."

I now visit in many classrooms to share my stories and poems and to inspire students and teachers to write about the world they know best — the world inside their classrooms. Everywhere I go, teachers and students tell me the most incredible stories. Sometimes they are laughing so hard, they can hardly get them out.

There was the sixth-grade teacher who told me of the class field trip to a highrise building. She loaded an elevator with twelve of her students and can you guess? Yes! The elevator became stuck between floors with the children inside. "You should have heard the screaming," she told me. "I wanted to crawl home, and forget the day ever happened."

Now imagine being trapped in an elevator with eleven of your peers? What would it be like? How would you feel? What would you do? Would there be anything funny about the experience? The questions are endless, as are the writing opportunities.

I once shared my poem "There's a Cobra in the Bathroom" with a fourth-grade class and its teacher. After I had read the poem, the teacher said, "Once I was teaching reading and I really did see a snake slithering on the floor right in my classroom."

I gasped. She had *lived* my story.

"What did you do when you saw the snake?" I asked.

"I raced out of the classroom," she replied.

"What about your students?"

"I left them," she said. "I went to get help, but I must confess that I did leave the children in the classroom — and I even closed the door behind me."

We laughed our way through this story, too, and then discovered that nearly all the children in the class had snake stories they wanted to share.

Once a teacher told me a story that brought her great joy. She arrived at school on a dark, dreary Friday morning. When she entered the hallway to walk to her classroom, she felt as cold as the wind that was blowing outside. From the far end of the hall, she saw one of her students, clutching a red flower in her hand.

"That rose," she told me, "made all the difference in my day!"

We are surrounded by moments of pure joy in our classrooms. We simply need to don the artist's lenses and start seeing and appreciating them, both for ourselves and for our students.

Oral language — starting point for writing

Children use magnificent imagery to express their deepest feelings. Often, one of their statements became the title and main idea of a poem.

Ben, a second grader, was scrounging around in a heap of coats and boots looking for a missing running shoe. Earlier that morning, he had lost his sweater, his schoolbag and his homework. The missing running shoe was the final straw. "There's a robber in our classroom," he told me in sheer frustration.

Perhaps he was right. My next poem began:

There's a robber in our classroom
And he steals all my things,
My school bag disappeared today,
As if it sprouted wings.

I always encouraged my students to work neatly. I'm not talking about initial drafts of stories, but of basic everyday work in their notebooks. They soon complained that I expected their work to be "neater than neat." I could hear the rhythm in those words and wrote:

My grade three teacher was surely no treat,
He forced us kids to write, neater than neat,
I'll rip out your pages for you to repeat,
If you don't take the care to write, neater than neat.
All messy writing is now obsolete,
For I only mark work that is neater than neat.

I'll never forget the day a substitute teacher was trying to get the attention of a class of fifth graders. "Did you all remember to bring your belly buttons to school today?" she asked as she turned off the classroom lights.

There was silence. She certainly had everyone's attention. I could see the pictures forming in the students' minds in the pause before the laughter started. Another story was born.

The gift of imagination

I have always had a vivid imagination. When I returned to teaching and found myself surrounded by wonderful stories, my creative consciousness was constantly on overload. Not only was I looking at the stories for what they were as we experienced them, but I was also imagining "What might happen if...?"

I began sharing my flights of imagination with the children. One day, for example, my daughter refused to get dressed to go to kindergarten. I told her that if she didn't hurry up and get ready, I would turn her into a frog.

We had so much fun that morning that I continued this story at school. "If you children don't get your work done on time, I am going to turn you all into frogs."

We laughed and joked and imagined what it would be like to be a class of second-grade frogs.

Another day, many of the children finished eating their lunches early and were becoming bored and fidgety waiting for the slowpokes. Brian was taking all the milk cartons and turning them into a train. I stopped and asked, "What might happen if we had magic powders that could freeze all the people in this room, except us?"

"We could play all afternoon and not get in trouble," Sarah called.

"I could take every single milk carton in the room and make a giant train," Brian informed us.

"I wouldn't have to do all my boring report cards," I added, fervently wishing those powders really did exist.

From then on, we were always imagining. What if we all became little people? What if we went to a space museum and a rocket took off? What if children were in charge of schools? What if we took a field trip to a dinosaur museum and a dinosaur came to life.

As a result of these musings, not only did we begin to see the world as we experienced it, but we also began adding colors and textures of our own, creating imaginative landscapes that were thrilling to explore.

I have come to believe that the elementary school classroom is the perfect starting place for traveling across a rainbow. Children are not meant to live only in the world of here and now, the black-and-white world of many classrooms. They are meant to reach out, experiment and explore, to stretch their imaginations. And if we let the children guide us, we too will discover colors we never knew existed.

Asked what she would do if she were in charge of schools, Alicia wrote:

> *We'd have a river running through the school and we could have canoeing and kayaking lessons. We would have science there and collect specimens in our bathing suits.*

And Lauren wrote that she met a toad on her way to school who said, "I have a magic powder just for you."

> *So it gave me a pink powder. I put it in my backpack. When I got to school, I didn't want to do my English so I poured it onto my English paper, and the teacher said, "Well, let's not do our English today. Let's watch a movie." I was happy.*
>
> *I saw the toad again on the way home, and I thanked him for the powder. And the powder never ran out.*

How comforting, in an imaginary world, to have a way of getting rid of work when you find it overwhelming, or when you just don't feel like doing it.

I told some of my stories in Mrs. Miller's fourth-grade class — stories about classes of children turning into little people, frogs and balloons. When I returned later in the year to tell more stories, the children were ready with their own. "Boinging" was the favorite, created by their teacher. Whenever she wanted to get rid of a student who was misbehaving, she would simply push a button on her desk and would "boing" him or her out of the room. What teacher wouldn't give a month's salary for such a device!

Mrs. Miller also took her students for rides on the clouds in order to help them relax before standardized tests. They would return to the classroom through the slats in the venetian blinds.

At other times, they pretended to be invisible, driving everyone in the cafeteria crazy with their giggling. At first, Mrs. Miller said, only a few children would join her on these escapades but, each time, more children were inspired to go along.

It takes practice and work to keep imagination alive.

One day, we had a fire drill and Timothy walked very slowly out the door. I urged him to rush, but he replied, "It's just a fire drill." I wanted to capture that moment on paper, for Timothy and all the other students who didn't understand the significance of those drills. It was imagination that allowed me to take my story one step further.

Timothy is such a fool
About so many things,
He claims to have no fear at all,
Whenever the fire bell rings.
Let me tell you what he said,
Laughing in my face,
"You can run when the fire bell rings,
As if you're in a race.
But I won't rush one little bit,
For I am not afraid.
I know it is just a drill,
A stupid, dumb parade,
Of kids who leave the building,
When they hear that screeching sound,
I'll never be in such a rush,
To get on that playground."

You can imagine what happens to Timothy, the fool.

As the fire blazed and the flames soared,
My friend I could not see,
And nobody has found him yet,
We know where he must be.

The next time the fire bell rang, Timothy left quickly with the rest of us. At the back of his mind, he could now imagine, "What might happen if...? "

This tale had worked in another way as well. The children were beginning to look at a galaxy of new writing possibilities. I had led the way, by sharing the world of my own imagination.

Creative use of the imagination will help our students become critical thinkers and problem solvers prepared to exist in the complex, multi-dimensional world of the twenty-first century. Imagination will be needed everywhere in their adult lives. Every career I can think of — law, science, medicine, teaching, politics, writing, art, marketing, sales, police work — depends on the active use of this faculty. A firefighter, for example, must imagine the best ways of dealing with the flames in order to fight the fire effectively. And it is critical reasoning skills that allow us, as teachers, to plan effective programs for our students. Even in our personal lives, the ability to imagine solutions to problems is critical to healthy development.

When I started imagining with my students, I realized how few adult models they had for doing this. Though they registered shock at first, they later relaxed and delighted in the stories. Once they knew my imagination was as crazy as theirs, they felt free to let their own loose.

In the beginning, I might have agreed with anyone who said that there is little educational value in activities like this. I too thought we were imagining just for the fun of it! But after researching the area, I have discovered that the active use of the imagination plays a vital role in all education.

We live in a society that prepackages imagination, and then dishes out exactly the same meal to each of us. Through television, movies, video games, after-school programs and structured teaching materials, children often have little room to develop their imaginative capacities.

In her article "On Imagination" published in *The Horn Book*, Joan Aiken wrote, "Seriously, I believe there should be imagination classes in every school — teaching children to use their own wits to amuse themselves, to keep themselves hopeful, to solve apparently insoluble problems, to try and get inside other people's personalities, to envisage other periods of time, other places, other states of being."

As teachers, we must lead the way by keeping our own imaginations alive and growing. There are many ways we can do this:

- By reading imaginative stories, poems and tales with children — taking them for a ride in the clouds.
- By continuously examining our school world and asking, "What might happen if...?"
- By searching out the extraordinary in the ordinary.
- By thinking about and discussing ways we can use our imagination to help solve everyday problems.
- By attempting, ourselves, to see the world in unaccustomed ways and then sharing our visions.

One day at lunch, Annie, a second grader, drank so much, we wondered what would happen to her. We took this real incident, sprinkled it with our imaginative powders and presto — we had a poem that is half true, half fantasy.

She drank all her milk
And an extra pint too,
Three glasses of grape juice,
Four of orange juice,
And one hundred and two slurps
From the water fountain.
I warned her to stop,
"You'll float away,
If you drink anymore."
She just laughed,
And drank all the juice,
In Frank's giant thermos,
And then asked Ben,
If he wanted all his milk.
That afternoon,
In the middle of a story,
We heard a gurgling sound,
And Annie started to float,
As if an ocean were underneath her.

She sailed right by Ms. Madison,
Over the desks,
Through the open door,
And down the hall.
We ran to watch Annie,
Float past the principal's office
And out the main door of our school.
Then she just floated away,
Like a ship at sea.

She should have listened to me.

Sharing our experiences

I should have known that the children would eventually want to dramatize the poems and stories we were sharing. When I wrote "Squirt! Squirt! On the Teacher's Skirt," we had a great time with a water gun and role-playing activities. On other occasions, we also acted out "Happy Hiccup to You" and "The Perfect Class."

When I wrote "Budging Lineups," I described what often happens as our children stand in straight lines to be marched from room to room.

Brenda stood in front of Ted,
Then Gregg budged in ahead of Fred.
Jackie yelled, "You're in my way.
Why do you do this every day?"
Then Jennifer cried that Joe budged in
To stand near his friend, Benjamin.

The poem continues until the last two lines, which read:

Ms. Jones sadly shook her head
Today she wished she'd stayed in bed.

After hearing this poem, the children pleaded, "Can we act it out?" It wasn't until later that I realized the significance of their request.

For them, this was the dream of Broadway. It also meant our language arts program had come full circle. By producing these poems and stories as theatrical pieces, we were sharing our experiences in the same way adults share theirs in theatre. We had written stories that began with our own life experiences, sprinkled them with imaginative powders and then rewritten them for a dramatic production.

It was easy and great fun to create our play "A Year in the Life of a Third-Grade Class." We selected our poems and stories, keeping in mind our audience and space and time limitations. While the children wrote most of the poems and stories themselves, they also borrowed others from the collection I was working on and from contemporary writers whose work we had come to enjoy.

The children divided into groups for their presentations. Our short poems and stories were very easy to handle in this context. Each group was responsible for the props, costumes, makeup, scenery and dialogue needed to complete its part of the presentation.

The children were thrilled with this production, though at the time I really didn't understand why. As with so many other aspects of this approach, my understanding would come with time.

I do remember meeting a man wearing a three-piece suit and toting an impressive briefcase in the halls of our school one morning. He was also carrying a paper bag.

"I wondered if you could tell me where the third graders are practicing their plays?" he asked. "My son, Benjamin, told me I had to deliver these worms by eleven o'clock."

I told him I was on my way to the theatre and would deliver the bag to Benjamin. I remember laughing as I walked down the hall and looked inside the bag. It was filled with candy worms, and I knew it was for the poem Benjamin was performing. The children are taking these productions awfully seriously, I thought to myself.

Angelo was another student in the third-grade class. He was a severe behavior problem, and often left school whenever he felt like it. His parents and teachers were at their wits' end trying to figure out what to do with this child.

During the third week of our drama unit, the classroom teacher reported that Angelo's attendance had been perfect for the entire time we had been working on our plays. We both knew he loved what he was doing, but we hadn't fathomed how much.

"Why?" I began to wonder. "What is the magic in these activities that sparks such a wholehearted response?"

I now realize these activities allowed my students to play. There was very little teacher interference, for the children worked with each other designing, structuring and producing their stories. Their imaginations were in high gear as they created costumes and scenery and searched for the props and words that would be most effective.

"We definitely need more old-fashioned playtime in our classes," I thought. "What better way to stimulate imaginations?"

The excitement backstage on the opening night of a Broadway production can't be more intense than that generated by this class of third graders, ready to share the experiences of their school year with parents, teachers and other classes.

I'll never forget the performance — the bright, shining faces of the children, the laughter of the parents and the amazement of the children in the audience as they realized how hysterically funny the elementary school world can be.

I had no fears that Angelo would leave in the middle of this performance; he arrived well ahead of time, anxious and excited. Benjamin's worms were perfect, and the entire audience gasped as he reached inside the bag to eat one. Of course, he hadn't told them they were candy worms.

For me, it was an enlightening experience. I knew the elementary school world could be exciting and dynamic, if only we took the time to explore beyond the textbooks and daily assignments. But, I never realized the stories could be captured on paper, spiced with a little imagination and performed so they could bring laughter and joy to an entire audience.

This was the world we shared in our classrooms every single day. Our writings and dramatic productions let us look at that world in such a way that we found its spice and flavor and, above all, came to appreciate its worth.

I'll never forget Caleb, playing himself in "Caleb's Desk is a Mess." We watched Jennifer, as his teacher, take all kinds of horrible things out of his desk — an old ham sandwich that was turning green, five monstrous spit wads, one sock with a hole in the toe, papers and notebooks that looked like they had been through the garbage disposal and the subtraction sheet Caleb thought Julian had stolen from him the week before. We watched her put the decaying pieces into a garbage bag, wash her hands and exclaim, "We have to help him get more organized!"

I laughed because I remembered precisely when this happened and Caleb's exact words when he came back to find his desk so neat and tidy. "Who ruined my desk? Now I'll never be able to find anything!"

Later I found out that Caleb's mother, who was sitting in the audience, had not been overly impressed with this production. "Why broadcast my son's messy desk?" she had asked.

I think Lucy Calkins gives us the answer: "Because this is (Caleb's) story."

Our classrooms are filled with the joy and wonder of life — if only we can see through the ordinary to the magic that is always there.

The need to be heard

In *The Art of Teaching Writing*, Lucy Calkins says, "...we will care about writing when it is personal and interpersonal. Beneath layers of resistance, we have a primal need to write. We need to make our truths beautiful and we need to say to others, 'This is me. This is my story, my life, my truth.' We need to be heard."

I hadn't realized how deeply these poems and stories were affecting my students, how they were giving the children a voice for the feelings, emotions, problems and joys of their world, the elementary school world. Their writings and dramatizations allowed my students to be heard.

When they wrote poems about being in charge of schools, for example, I learned a great deal about them. They consistently requested more food, more exercise, and less tedious work.

If kids were put in charge of schools,
We'd let the teachers get paid for not teaching,
We'd have recess every half hour,
We'd ride scooters in the halls,
We'd build an arena in the school and wrestle there.
We'd probably start World War III,
We'd have all kinds of breaks for food,
Like pizza, popcorn and ice cream.
We'd have gym for ten hours of the day,
And only go to school one day of the week.

Once, I wrote a story called "A Lifetime in Third Grade." It was written near the end of the school year, after a long discussion with a group of third graders who had been receiving remedial help. They all thought they were going to fail (I knew they were) and were preparing themselves for the repercussions.

"My mom is going to make me live with my dad if I fail," John told me.

"That's nothing compared to my problem," said Sarah. "My parents are going to send me back to Chile, and I don't want to go."

"I'll be in summer school all day, and I'll have to do homework all night," groaned Jimmy. "And I've looked forward to summer all year."

I could feel the despair in these words and I think I captured it in my story, about a child who *does* spend his entire life in the third grade. He never goes on to the next grade, even though he watches generations of children pass into and out of the school. The poem ends:

And when the world ends,
And all the stories have been told,
They'll say,
"Poor Josh,
He was the only person,
In the history of the world,
Who spent a lifetime in third grade."

After writing this story, I put it away in the bottom drawer of my filing cabinet because I thought it was far too depressing to share with the children. Several weeks later, however, I took it out, read it again and laughed. I began reading it to my classes and in other schools — nearly everywhere, in fact — and it soon became a favorite.

After some reflection, I realized this poem voiced the students' worst fears in a humorous way.

In his song "Hey There, Mr. Lonely Heart," John Denver writes that his dream is for us to share "all we have and all we see." I like these words, for when we ask our children to write about the school world, we are asking them to share "all they have and all they see."

Danny, a first grader, wrote a short piece telling me about life on the playground. I love the title — "Kissy, Kissy"!

Drew and I play kissy girls.
We sometimes chase girls on the playground.
But we don't really kiss them.
We just like to chase each other around.

Another first grader, Sandra, shared with me an event that had just happened in her classroom.

Once I brought my hamster to school. His name was
Harry and he made a mess.
"You will not come with me again because you got me in
trouble, Harry."
He started crying. I told him I was sorry.

Our children need a voice, to understand their own experiences and to share their hopes and dreams.

One day, Jennie was working frantically on her reading activities, trying to get them completed as quickly as possible.

I knew Jennie could write neatly and take care with her work. But every day she raced to complete it. I finally asked why and wrote her answer in the poem "My Writing is an Awful Mess."

My writing is an awful mess,
And my teacher asked me why,
"I work fast to get it done,"
I told her with a sigh.
"I want to finish all my work,

So I can talk with friends,
It's much too long to have to wait,
Until the school day finally ends.
I never check my spelling,
Punctuation I don't try,
For if I spent my time on these,
My social life would die.
It's talking with my friends each day,
That keeps my whole world bright,
And I don't want to give it up,
Just to get my work all right."

A voice for those feelings!"

During recess, the second-grade boys always chased the second-grade girls. Don't ask me how, but one day a girl ended up as the co-leader of the boys' team. She was called a traitor by some of the other girls. This story has led to many fascinating discussions:

When the boys chase the girls and the girls chase the boys,
Why can't a girl be the leader of the boys?

Not only were we able to celebrate the special moments in our classroom but, through the written word, we were being heard. The stories and poems gave us a chance to hold a little bit of life in our hands, so we could look at it carefully, understand it and then share it with those most important to us.

Initiating this approach

I can only share with you how I developed this approach and, as I've said before, I did it without even realizing I was doing so. When I returned to teaching after my years as a writer, I found stories everywhere. The elementary school world hadn't changed, but I had. The stories had, in fact, always been there.

I have tried walking into classrooms, sharing poetry and then inviting the children to write their own. This approach can be very effective: on occasion, some students have completed poems before I even finish my presentation.

But I feel that the greatest source of inspiration is teachers who model the behavior of a real writer. They show children, through their own example, how an artist looks at life, takes in all the dimensions he or she can see, and then transforms it into a work of art.

The beginning step for teachers is to slow down, step off the fast-paced carousel of curriculum goals and objectives, and take time to really see what is going on in the classroom. We need to spend more time talking with students, asking their opinions and soliciting their comments about life. We need to be on the lookout for special moments that can be transformed into special stories.

Poetry sings for me and comes easily, but it is not essential to be able to write it. Instead, a teacher might choose to write letters to his or her students.

Dear Students,

I have something I would like to share with you. Every day, when I stand up at the front of the classroom and talk to you, I watch your faces to see if you are listening. In the beginning, everyone is usually listening, but as time goes on and you find my words a little boring, you start reaching inside your desks for things.

Yesterday, I saw trucks, cars, erasers and even a running shoe slip out of your desks as I explained the rules for field day. I knew it was time to stop when I saw a student pull out a toothbrush and toothpaste. I wondered if he planned to brush his teeth right there!

I'll try and keep my lectures short, but please do your best to listen.

Wouldn't it be awful if you were sitting in a college-level class one day and became so bored that you pulled out a musical instrument and started playing it?

Your professor would yell, "Didn't you learn anything in all your years of school?"

I would feel very badly if I thought I hadn't taught you how important listening is.

Please do your best. I know it isn't easy to listen all the time and I'll do my best to keep my lectures as short as possible.

Yours truly,
Your Teacher.

You can also model the kinds of stories that can be written, based on real classroom events. Perhaps, for example, a group of children have failed a reading test. You could write a story that simply describes their behavior.

The children sat with gloomy looks on their faces. It felt as if it had started raining right in their very own classroom.
Sandra squished up her paper and threw it in the garbage. Betty checked hers over carefully, to see if the teacher forgot to add some marks to her score. Eric ripped his in one-hundred little pieces and put the pieces at the bottom of his book bag. And Dick folded his paper neatly and put it inside his reading book.
Sarah said, "I hate these dumb reading tests anyway."
It is never easy to fail a test.

Here's another example to model:

I was walking down the hall after my lunch break, when I saw seven of my students racing down the hallway like rabbits from Alice in Wonderland.
I wondered what the rush was all about. Were they racing to be the first to class? Were they racing because they could hardly wait to get more work to do? Were they racing because they knew they would get a detention if they were caught?
Now I'm sitting at my desk and really wondering why my students were racing down the hall.

These examples are all common occurrences in elementary schools. But they become special when we write about them. In this way, we begin to share our emotions and feelings, our wonder and curiosity with each other, and we get to the heart of what is really going on in our students' lives.

In a speech delivered to the International Reading Association's annual conference in Toronto, Lucy Calkins suggested that our classrooms have become "emotionally neutral." By dealing with the very human experiences of our children through these stories, we bring emotions back into the classroom, exposing them to the light where they can be seen and understood.

Words of caution

- In order to screen out potentially hurtful comments, it may be a good idea for the teacher to read the children's writings before they are shared with the class.

- Teachers may decide they wish their students to use fictional names. At the very least, it may be wise to discuss the moral problems of writing about other class members.

- Sometimes, a child who is extremely angry or depressed may use this medium to express his or her thoughts and feelings. Certainly, teachers should report severe cases for counseling.

Sharing your stories

A variety of techniques can be used to create and preserve the memories of the year spent with your students. Children especially enjoy working in pairs or small groups to produce these works.

- Publishing individual books.

- Publishing anthologies of stories. Classroom stories and illustrations might be collected in one book. This book quickly became a favorite in my classrooms as students read and reread their stories hundreds of times.

- Big books. My students had great fun turning their poems and stories into big books to share with other classes. Sometimes we all wrote on the same topic, with each child contributing one sentence and one illustration.

- Dramatizations. Performing the stories was the odds-on favorite in all my classes.

- Group stories. When something happens in the classroom, invite the children to describe it in a poem, story, article or letter written with you. In this kind of language experience activity, the teacher can model some of his or her own writing behaviors. This is a good time to practice the "What might happen if...?" technique that is so important for stimulating imaginations.

- Journals and diaries. These are a wonderful way to remember a year together. A private diary, where students record their daily lives, is also a good idea. The children may give the teacher permission to read their entries, but this is not mandatory. In this way, they are given freedom to use writing as an outlet for venting emotions and feelings, a tool for understanding their daily lives and an aid in celebrating and coping with life.

Whole language and personal growth

This kind of writing is very important because it embraces our humanity. By providing words for the thoughts and feelings we experience, it helps us grow as human beings and relish the joy of sharing life. We gain the insight to understand that we are all alike at the most fundamental level.

This is what whole language is all about. It is language used for the growth of children in the most complete sense, language that services children in their day-to-day world, language that is a medium for celebrating life, and language that accepts children as they are today and lays the foundations for healthy growth tomorrow.

By writing about our lives, we begin to understand what it means to be human. We learn to see more, feel more, think more, care more and imagine more. When we leave our own world behind to explore other cultures and other lands, each adventure brings us back to ourselves — but to stronger, healthier selves, who are learning to pull together the connections of understanding.

All that's left is the story

My writing experiences led me to a realization that has changed how I look at my students, my teaching career and life in general. I've come to see that I am writing the most important chapters of my life, in all its simple, routine interactions. Every day at school, from the moment I arrive until I pull on my coat to leave for home, my students are the characters who live and create the plots with me.

"All the world's a stage and all the men and women merely players," wrote William Shakespeare. The elementary school world makes a marvelous stage for writing and theatrical possibilities.

There's a wonderful story called *White Wave*. At the end, people have died and the author, Diane Wolkstein, says, "But that is how it is with all of us: When we die, all that remains is the story."

Let us value and treasure the stories that make up the chapters of our school lives. I can't think of anything more tragic than missing our own story.

Bibliography

Aiken, Joan. "On Imagination" in *The Horn Book*. November/December, 1984.

Calkins, Lucy McCormick. *The Art of Teaching Writing*. Heinemann, 1986.

Wolkstein, Diane. *White Wave*. Crowell, 1979.

Paterson, Katherine. *Gates of Excellence, On Reading and Writing Books for Children*. Elsevier/Nelson, 1981.

Pearsall, Paul. *Super Joy*. Doubleday, 1988.

Titles in the New Directions series

Each book in the New Directions series deals with a single, practical classroom topic or concern, teaching strategy or approach. Many teachers have recognized the collegial and encouraging tone in them — not surprising, since most of them have been written by practicing teachers. Indeed, if you have an idea for a New Directions title of your own, we encourage you to contact the Publishing Division, Scholastic Canada.

Existing titles include:

Borrow-a-Book: Your Classroom Library Goes Home	Linda Hart-Hewins Jan Wells
Classroom Drama: Act It Out	Gare Thompson
Evaluation: Whole Language, Whole Child	Jane Baskwill Paulette Whitman
A Guide to Classroom Publishing	Jane Baskwill Paulette Whitman
Literature-Based Learning: One School's Journey	Fran Buncombe Adrian Peetoom
Shared Reading: Safe Risks with Whole Books	Adrian Peetoom
A Teacher's Guide to Shared Reading	Frank Barrett
Using Big Books and Predictable Books	Priscilla Lynch
What's There to Write About?	Kalli Dakos
A Whole Language Primer	Lee Gunderson

In Canada, order from: Scholastic-TAB Publications Ltd., 123 Newkirk Road, Richmond Hill, ON L4C 3G5.

In the United States, order from: Scholastic Inc., Box 7502, Jefferson City, MO 65102.